The ration

Unde oung Peop church and How to Help Them Stay

Laurence Singlehurst

Director, Cell UK

Laura Hancock

Director, British Youth for Christ

GROVE BOOKS LIMITED

RIDLEY HALL RD CAMBRIDGE CB3 9HU

Contents

Note

This booklet is split into two parts. The first—written by Laurence Singlehurst out of his experience with young people through the work of Youth with a Mission (YWAM), his involvement with universities through doing missions and subsequently being on the board of Fusion—outlines why we might be losing so many young people to church attendance. The second part—written by Laura Hancock, a director at British Youth for Christ who has written Christian curricula for a number of years—provides a possible curriculum for churches to consider in their youth work.

First Impression December 2019
ISSN 1748-3492
ISBN 978 1 78827 107 3

1 Introduction

The purpose of this Grove booklet is to look at a crisis that has been developing and growing within the context of church for many years. In simple terms, this relates to young people who grow up in church, seem to have an experience of God, and yet by the time they reach 24 have drifted from church attendance and possibly from faith itself.

It is perhaps hard to prove conclusively how high this percentage drop-off is. All the time I was involved in working with young people, it was quoted as being 50%. Recent research seems to show that this statistic remains very high. *The 'No Religion' Population of Britain*, research by Stephen Bullivant of St Mary's University, Twickenham, seems to indicate that for every one convert we are losing what he calls 26 'nonverts' who were existing members of the faith community.[1] Because most converts as shown by the Christian mapping research are under the age of 25 we can assume that this is lots of Christian young people. If we look experientially at our own family and wider families with young people who grew up in strong Christian families, we see quite a number of these young people no longer attend church and this would seem to confirm these statistics.

For every one convert we are losing 26 'nonverts'

As the church in England becomes more missional and we are reaching out purposefully it seems to me that, if we are putting a huge amount of effort, time and money into winning new folk, then we ought to look again at the elephant in the room and ask ourselves a question about these young people, many of whom we are losing from church from about the age of 18.

It is not the purpose of this booklet to lay blame in any way whatsoever. It is not pointing at church leaders, youth leaders, families or even the young people themselves. It is just saying, 'We have a problem.' In the immortal words of the astronaut—'Houston, we've had a problem!'

It is also the purpose of this booklet to say that we are doing very well with those who do not leave church and we can learn from what has helped to keep their faith alive and active. In this booklet, we will see what we can learn from both the bad news and the good news and hope it will give us some solutions to the challenge we face.

2

Matching Experience with Understanding

For many years, the Parable of the Sower has been an inspiration to me. In my book, *Sowing, Reaping, Keeping,* I pointed out that the Parable of the Sower is about understanding how the seed which is the word of God develops in people's lives or how it does not develop in people's lives.[2] Where there is a lack of understanding of the word we are shown that in the path which represents hard soil the word does not develop at all. In the rocky soil the word develops for a while then hard times crush it. In the thorny soil which is also mixed with good soil it flourishes for what could be quite a long period of time and is then choked by the thorns and thistles. So there are consequences to the individuals' walk of faith. As I began to think about a lost generation, I was drawn back to this parable. It is a parable that describes the journey of the sowing of the word in people's lives and the possible outcomes. We see in this parable one positive outcome and three negatives.

Creating Good Soil

What does it take for the soil to be good? This is what we want to find out, so what are the ingredients of the good soil? This parable gives us two ingredients for the good soil. In Luke 13.18 the parable tells us that the good soil has an honest heart. In Matthew 13 we see the principle of understanding, therefore the listeners understand by implication both the benefits and the cost, and they bear fruit. So, to put that in contemporary language, they have positive experiences, they understand both the benefits and the cost of faith, hence they bear fruit. In other words we want Christian young people to have positive experiences of God, his kingdom, his church. We want them to understand the real components of Christian faith, the character of God, surrender, the life lived out, the world they live in, a positive view of themselves. Also, as is reasonable to expect of a young person, they have been involved in Christian service: loving their neighbour, sharing their faith. My experience is that where I see young people who have flourished in their faith, these components of experience, understanding and service are evident in their lives.

We want Christian young people to have positive experiences of God, his kingdom, his church

My experience in Youth with a Mission confirmed this. I pay tribute to Loren Cunningham, who founded YWAM and wrote a curriculum for a discipleship training school in the early 1970s. It is estimated that since 1974 over 1 million people have attended a discipleship training school and it has been highly successful in terms of its discipleship impact and the grounding of young people in faith. It consists of a 12-week lecture phase that covers a curriculum of understanding and within the context of that understanding there is a significant amount of Christian experience through small groups, through ministry and through prayer. These 12 weeks are followed by another 12 weeks of outreach and volunteer work, of Christian service, loving the lost and caring for those in need. Now it is not a perfect programme and not all the young people do well. But a very significant percentage are helped to stay in faith and are still attending church in their 20s.

Faith Choked by Thorns

The metaphor of the good soil tells us that proper understanding of the dynamics of Christian faith is very important. So what can we learn from the other soils? I particularly want to focus on the third of the soils. Matthew 13.22 says: 'This is what was sown among the thorns, these are those who hear the word, but the cares of the world and the delight in riches which draws them away and the word becomes unfruitful.' It is particularly important that we think about this verse in the context of our young people. In my opinion this verse tells us that the cares, the joys of the world, the delight in riches creep in over a period of time and eventually choke the word. This is what we see happen with our young people. They progress through the life of church through a number of years but from about 16 onwards life begins to creep in. Their foundations are not strong enough and the word of faith is choked.

This is having more impact today than was true of Christians who grew up in the 1950s and 1960s because they grew up with a remnant of Christian worldview and the culture still had a Christian moral foundation and plumb line. In the charismatic movement and contemporary church, we had powerful spiritual experiences. Understanding and experience together proved to be a strong foundation that helped us stand against the cares of the world and the delight in riches. But today's context is unlike the previous generation.

My hypothesis is this: today's generation have grown up in a society where there is far less Christian understanding in our culture and their Christian life has largely been full of experiences—many positive, some negative. In their youth groups they have had experience of worship, salvation and charismatic experiences and much of our contemporary youth work has had a strong experiential focus. On top of this they have gone to great Christian conferences that give them huge experiential injections. Superficially, this all looks good:

we have young people who can worship, who seem to really love Jesus, and yet, I believe, this masks a fundamental problem. They do not get enough understanding of who God is, his goodness and character, of what is the real essence of salvation. Nor do they build a real view of themselves and a real view of what the world is really like.

We have assumed that they will absorb, through their Christian families and church attendance, the necessary understanding that will give them the foundations they need. But this may be a misconceived idea.

Christian Experience, Secular Worldview

Judith Harris, author of *The Nurture Assumption,* is a radical American sociologist who basically says that young people are not shaped by their genetics and family background, but they are shaped by their friends and peer groups.[3] Their worldview is the worldview of their peer group which is stronger than parental influence. This worldview is secular and postmodern. Our culture has moved away from a Christian understanding of right and wrong in pursuit of ethics based on human reason and emotion. Secularism is redefining right and wrong and we have a generation that is characterized for its tolerance and liberalism where the only thing that is wrong is to say you are right. It is the hypothesis of this book that this is what young people absorb. So you end up with Christian experience, sitting on a secular worldview, which to start with seems a good foundation, but as young people grow older, a tsunami is approaching. This tsunami begins to manifest itself in their late teens when many of their unchurched friends are experiencing the pleasures of this world and we begin to get young people living in two worlds at once—their church world and the rest of their lives.

Young people have the capacity of two cultures: their background and their friends

Judith Harris explains that young people have the capacity of two cultures—a subculture, which is the culture of their background, in this case, the church, and a dominant culture, which is the culture of their friends. Her hypothesis is that young people do not become rebellious, they just learn to live in two cultures. They are happy with their friends. Then they come into their church life, lay the peer-group culture down, pick up their background culture, and shout 'Hallelujah Jesus,' both in the youth group and in the church. Many of us have seen this capacity to live in two worlds, with very little conscience, and been somewhat bemused by it. I call this 'enthusiastic dualism.'

Harris goes on to say that, as they then approach their late teens and early 20s they experience the full impact of the tsunami. This is also amplified through the increased number going to university. We all know that, whether in university or just hanging out with your friends in your early 20s, every experience is on offer in a way that for many of us of an older generation seems completely unbelievable. If you sit down with the honest young person who has been through university life and ask them to tell you what is on offer, what they have experienced, you may be shocked.

The sad reality is this: our young people are not prepared for this. Their Christian experience, based on a secular worldview, is not strong enough to keep them in faith. Too many questions are raised about the goodness and character of God. Too many questions about justice and pain in the world. Their foundations are not strong enough to answer these questions and this causes, in some, unresolved questions that are part of the reason they begin to drift away Too many experiences are on offer. They are old enough to reflect on their background. When my friend asked his daughter why she no longer attends church, despite having had a great youth group and positive experiences in Christianity, she said, 'I don't understand.' She did not have the foundations that were necessary not only to have great Christian experiences but to understand the foundations of faith that must go alongside these experiences.

If this young lady did not truly understand what Christian faith really meant in today's context, then I think that we, the body of Christ, have to take some responsibility for this. Making sure that people understand the key components of faith, as well as Christian experience, is our responsibility.

3 Lessons from Those Who Remain

We have looked at the impact that the cares of the world and the delight in riches can have on the faith of young people. However, before we move on from this parable we might want to reflect a little bit more on the good soil. The statistics encourage us that a significant number of Christian young people do not lose their faith. They attend church into adult life and in that regard the church is doing well. So we might want to highlight some factors that explain why this group is thriving.

One of these factors can be learnt from Judith Harris's research. Just as our young people can take a secular worldview from their school friends and media they can also be influenced by positive Christian peer input. This positive Christian peer influence can take two forms. The first is good peer explanation of faith, which creates the understanding we have talked about. The second is through a peer demonstration of lifestyle that shows positive Christian character through peer relationships.

Jesus teaches his disciples and is a positive peer model

This model is the Jesus approach. Jesus is asking his disciples to follow him and in that experience of following him he does two things. One: he teaches them, they have amazing experiences, and yet it is all fully earthed in the life and teaching of Jesus. Two: he is a positive peer model to his disciples. So not only is this the hypothesis of Judith Harris, that negative and positive peers have a real impact for us; this is enshrined in Jesus' command to follow him and in the whole sense of being a disciple.

Positive Peer Influence

It is interesting to note, going back to the Youth with a Mission example, that Barry Austin, one of the shapers of Loren Cunningham's discipleship training idea, realized that this peer concept was important. He created small groups that the students belonged to, that were led by a peer. Small group leaders spent a great deal of time with the people in their small group. You then have in this model the teacher in the lecture programme, who is often of another generation, and the small group leader who is a peer to those people on the course. I think this is a very key component to the success of the YWAM idea.

It is seen in a number of other models of similar courses that demonstrate its success.

But we can go to another place to substantiate this idea. If you speak to a 20-year old, a 26-year old or a 50-year old who is walking positively in faith and you ask them about their early days, many will talk about a peer figure who was a positive example to them at that time.

I remember a group of young 16- to 20-year olds, all of them involved in a very positive Christian environment and most of them beginning to live in two worlds at once. It was perceived by the group's leaders that there was a problem, and rightly there was much preaching, praying and challenging of these young people. All of this effort did not seem to make the impact we had hoped it would. However one day a young 22-year old, who was a peer age to this group, turned up. This young man was very much grounded in his faith but he looked like these young people and he was of their culture. He teamed up with his older brother, who was about 9 years his senior, and between them they began to challenge these young people. Uniquely for that moment they did not just offer Christian experience but they taught them the fundamentals of faith, which were demonstrated in the lives of these two brothers. The impact on these 20 young people was extraordinary. Nineteen of them, now all in their mid-30s, are actively involved in church.

From 1995 a number of churches around the country who had seen the importance of positive peer leadership created small groups within their youth work. These were often led by a peer—a 17-year old or a 16-year old. These small groups also provided not only a dynamic positive peer influence but to make them work there had to be a measure of curriculum and intentionality. I think this was a very positive example and something that churches would do well to consider in our ongoing challenge of positive peer influence.

So for these young people, whether it was through the main church services and *Youth Alpha* (or similar), or through their youth workers or family, our hypothesis is that there was more intentionality in the teaching they received. Those core issues of curriculum we have mentioned, and will mention further, have been put in place.

A number of years ago, I had the pleasure of hearing Dr Ralph Neighbour speak, whose books on discipleship within the American Baptist denomination have sold over a million copies.[4] He was always clear, as a preacher and an educator, that there need to be clear pathways and clear curricula, and his preference was that it was done through a book or a resource, so it had some objectivity to it. But I am sure there are many ways of communicating clear biblical principles about God and the Christian life.

4

The Renewed Mind

In Rom 12.2, the apostle Paul tells us, 'Do not be conformed to this world, but be transformed by the renewing of your mind, that you may prove what is the will of God, what is good, acceptable and perfect.'

It is quite clear here that the apostle Paul and the early church understood that there had to be a change of worldview. Whether it was changing a worldview of Greco-Roman philosophy or pagan philosophy to Christian, things needed to shift. The early church dealt with this issue through catechism and for some it would take them two to three years to go through catechism before they entered into the fullness of church life. The doorway into that pathway of catechism may have been a conversion experience of some sort. There have been other times too in the history of the church where it has been seen to have been important that through creeds and other intentional methods, including hymns, opportunities were taken to give positive Christian content and an understanding of faith to new converts.

In today's world psychologists tell us that our beliefs shape our values, our values shape our actions. Often as Christians we focus on actions—do this, do that, do not do this, do not do that. But if the young people do not have the correlating beliefs and values that relate to those actions, they will change their behaviour in the moment perhaps, but revert back to whatever their belief and values tell them. So the renewing of the mind, the catechism of the early church was a way to make sure that these new Christians who grew up in a pagan culture would adopt Christian beliefs and values that would correspondingly impact their choices. That is what we must do today. We must make sure that young people have the correct beliefs and values which become the foundation of their actions.

We must make sure that young people have the correct beliefs and values

In today's postmodern culture it will be no surprise to us that the church in America has been grappling with these issues for some while. Nancy Pearcey, in her book, *Finding Truth,* suggests that youth groups fail young Christians intellectually but are often good at getting an emotional commitment. Her book challenges the mind-set of 'Don't think, just believe,' whether in the church, the classroom, the media or politics.[5] David Kinnaman, in his book, *You Lost Me,* based on the Barna Group research, puts across the same kind of argument.[6] Their survey showed that less than one half of one per cent of Christians in America between the ages of 18–23 has a biblical worldview.

Softening the Tone

Another study by Fuller Seminary determined that the most important factor in whether young people left the church or remained steadfast in their faith, was whether they had a safe haven to express their doubts and concerns regarding the Scriptures and their faith before leaving home.[7] What this says to us, is that it is not only about ensuring that a Christian worldview, a curriculum of ideas is covered, it is the style of how that is delivered and the tone of voice. The historic tone of voice here in the UK, and I have no doubt in the US, has been the authoritative voice. When we have put across Christian ideas about God and life, it has been in a 'this is the truth voice, take it or leave it.' Unfortunately, this tone of voice is all about hearing, but not necessarily understanding. Real understanding has to be in a safe environment, where I can raise my questions, however shocking they may appear, and I am not seen as a rebel or a doubter and we welcome the dialogue. So our tone of voice needs to be propositional. This is what we think. This is why we think it. How do you see it?

Real understanding has to be in a safe environment, where I can raise my questions, however shocking

A British Christian leader, in talking to a youth group, contrasted a Christian worldview with the secular postmodern view of the world. He put it across in a propositional voice. At the end, one of the questions he asked was, 'What have you learned tonight?' One young man was very quick to stand to his feet and spoke out that he had understood that he was making his decisions, his lifestyle choices, based on a worldly view, and he was living in two worlds at once. That is the beginning of understanding, the start of a journey of self-discovery.

Josh McDowell, well known for his apologetics in the 1970s, said in a recent youth conference, 'When young people ask you a question, don't tell them the answer, ask them another question.' He was going a step further to say that the culture we need to create is a listening culture, one where dialogue is valued and encouraged.

Here in the UK, we need to realize that we have a problem. The statistics are clear. Our personal observations are clear. We want to continue to embrace positive Christian experience, but with a new intentionality to think about and encourage young people to understand a Christian worldview.

Engaging Church Leaders, Parents and Youth Workers

It is our hope that the curriculum ideas you will see in the next chapter would be held by church leaders, families and youth leaders. So our proposal is that these three groups of people could adopt a curriculum similar to the one we are suggesting in the next chapters. They could ask themselves what the eight to ten areas of understanding are that young people need to know about God, faith and the world around them and write their own curriculum. Wherever this curriculum comes from it could be adopted by these three stakeholders—church leaders, youth leaders and families. And through church on Sunday, through the youth group and lived out by the families and reinforced, these areas would be taught and experienced in different ways to different depths over a five-year period. Once a year the various stakeholders could come together and discuss how they feel this process of curriculum is developing, suggestions and tweaks could be considered and this would give a wonderful holistic approach to youth work, where youth workers do not feel isolated and on their own but everyone together takes on this awesome responsibility of helping our young people on their journey of faith.

As mentioned earlier the delivery of this curriculum is key, so thought needs to be given to how this is approached. The raising up of peer leaders for small groups could be one consideration here. Also, involving the young people in delivering some of the curriculum to the whole group may be appropriate. Giving space for exploration and raising doubts and concerns, as I have highlighted, is another crucial factor.

5

Why Use a Curriculum?

Young people of the current generation are growing up in a world unlike any before them. It is a generation that is more digitally connected than any before it, has greater exposure to marketing than any previous generation and is able to have most desires met almost immediately. They are taking on the stewardship of a planet on the brink of environmental meltdown and war and terrorism look different now to how they ever have before. For these young people today the terrain is shifting, and we must disciple young people in such a way that they are able to assess and navigate this change in landscape, whilst growing up to be passionate followers of Jesus.

Often, as youth leaders, our discipleship methods are reactive to the culture of the young people that we care for. For example, some of our young people are going through a difficult time so we run a few sessions on suffering or 'Where is God when things are tough?' Or maybe our young people all start flirting with each other, so we run a sex and relationships series in the hope that they read between the lines. The problem here is that we do not lay foundations for young people's development when we lead a reactive youth ministry rather than a pre-emptive one. Curriculum enables us to do that.

When young people come into our care, we hope to have them from the ages of 11–18 and for them to follow Jesus way beyond that. We should be creating an intentional journey for these young people so that they not only get to the destination that we desire, but are fully equipped for the somewhat uncharted journey that they are embarking on. If you consider setting out on a car journey you work out the destination before you leave, assess the terrain and adjust the car accordingly, programme your journey intentionally, not to mention making sure that your car is prepared for every eventuality along the way. This should be our attitude when discipling our young people, knowing where we want to take them, and no matter how the terrain or landscape changes for this generation, preparing them for the journey that they may face ahead of them.

How to Structure a Curriculum

We have been using a curriculum model since 2015, both in the resources that we create at Youth for Christ and in the youth work within our local church, and are beginning to see the fruits of young people travelling an intentional discipleship journey over time. In our resources at Youth for Christ we use six topics within our annual curriculum, but listed in the next chapter are a number of topics that you might want to consider if you are building a teaching curriculum of your own. If you would like to check out what we create and what this looks like in practice, please do visit the website where you can view some practical outworking of what we are talking through here.[8]

Once you have prayed and established what you believe to be the core content to your teaching curriculum, you can then establish a teaching structure and the guidelines around this. For example, at Youth for Christ, we teach into our six core topics for approximately a half-term each in every academic year, therefore each year, six key foundations are taught into in varied and creative ways. In theory, if a young person journeys through your youth ministry from the ages of 11–18 then they will receive seven or eight years of regular teaching on spiritual disciplines, healthy relationships, the person of Jesus, evangelism or whichever teaching topics you consider fundamental to a young person's spiritual development. It is important to note, however, that a curriculum you build should not be so regimented or legalistic that there is no space for deviation. We will often leave space within a half-term to be able to teach a miniseries or one-off sessions that can step away from the curriculum or follow the prompting of the Holy Spirit where needed.

The sessions should be journeying young people towards Jesus no matter where they are

Another principle that we use whilst creating sessions is that the sessions themselves should not only be rooted in the Bible but, through discipleship content, should journey young people towards Jesus no matter where they are at in their faith. This means that the content should be accessible to a young person if they have been to church their whole lives or if this is their first week. This affects the words we use, the explanations that we give, the topics that we cover and environment that we create for these sessions to take place in, but all of this begins with a solid foundation of regular content.

Creating a Curriculum

Within the next section of this booklet, we have sought to outline some curricula that you might want to consider when building your own youth ministry teaching, and also what the outworking of these topics might look like in a teaching environment or a youth group setting. Each of the sessions should be rooted in the Bible and be taught from appropriate passages but also relate to the issues that young people are facing today.

It is vitally important that we do not mindlessly repeat the same content year upon year, but creatively engage with our curriculum, bringing relevant issues, the Bible and the application and outworking of faith to life, so that young people might be able to consider these topics from different angles and learn how to apply them in a variety of settings as they develop into disciples who are themselves making disciples into their adult lives.

6 Sample Curricula

We are proposing eight areas to focus around and are offering curriculum outlines for each of these for you to follow. The areas are as follows:

1. Jesus-centred Living
2. Relationships
3. Giving and Serving
4. Sharing the Gospel
5. Living Wisely
6. Connecting with God
7. Character of God
8. Identity

For each area I have written a general introduction as a way of giving some background and context. This is then followed by a curriculum outline that highlights suggested areas for you to look at and develop. It will, of course, be essential that you work out the details of what specifically you include and how you teach depending on the young people you are working with. There are some really good resources available; be sure to make what you do interactive and use video clips wherever you can.

As we saw earlier, one of the main influencers for this age group are their peers, so make sure you engage peers in the delivery and preparation of the teaching. This could be in asking some of those in the group with leadership potential to share part of the teaching with you in, say, sharing an example of what this might look like for them. Another way to involve them is to have small discussion groups and ask them to lead the groups, having spent time with them yourself before the session, helping them prepare to lead the groups by sharing the teaching content with them and helping them formulate questions to lead the small group well.

1 Jesus-centred Living

This means to think about what it looks like to keep the person and teachings of Jesus at the centre of our lives. This might be at school, at home, with friends or wherever we are. The person of Jesus is the foundation of our faith and a Jesus-centred life affects what we do, what we say, how we live and how we view and love others. This theme encourages and challenges the young people to invite Jesus to be the centre of everything and take a look at the teaching and person of Jesus as they look to orientate their lives around him.

Curriculum for Teaching

The Historicity of Jesus

What is the evidence and truth behind the person of Jesus and whether he existed? Here you might work through the evidence that Jesus was who he says he was, or if he even existed at all. Sessions covering the evidence for Jesus' existence might include, was he born? Did he die and come back to life? What does the Old Testament say about him?

Study of a Gospel

This is an opportunity to conduct an in-depth study of one of the gospels. It might be that you want to pick four of five defining moments of Jesus' ministry, the 'I am' statements of John's gospel, or even compare and contrast the person of Jesus in the gospels themselves.

Close Encounters

Throughout the gospels Jesus had significant interactions with the people around him, and these told us not only about who Jesus is but also how he sees us. Select some of these interactions and unpack their significance. For example, the Roman centurion, Zacchaeus, the calling of his disciples, Peter's reinstatement, or an interaction with the religious teachers; use these examples to learn about Jesus and also about how we should treat others.

Beatitudes

Take your group on a journey through Matthew 5, selecting a number of the Beatitudes and what Jesus may have been getting at when he was talking about them. Apply these truths to the young people's current contexts and build a picture of not only who Jesus was, but also the kind of people that Jesus stood up for and died for, and how we might give our lives to do the same.

2 Relationships

Relationships are a key part of our lives. They can be good, bad, fun, difficult, enriching and much more! This theme unpacks topics like sex and relationships, families, friends and how we can have healthy relationships in the way that God intends us to.

Curriculum for Teaching

Sex and Relationships

This is something that young people really want to talk about, but often their youth leaders shy away from! If we as youth workers are not speaking into, and modelling, healthy relationships, then a young person's only source of education will be what they learn through surrounding media. One way of teaching into this area is by covering the four stages of a relationship and leading specific sessions around each stage: getting together, staying together, sex and breaking up well.

BFFs

BFFs stand for 'best friends forever.' In a world of connections and digital media, this theme gives opportunity to speak into modelling healthy relationships in different areas of young people's lives. This might be done through Bible studies around certain relationships, for example David and Jonathan modelling friendship, Ruth and Naomi modelling an older to younger relationship or Elijah and Elisha demonstrating a mentor–mentee relationship.

Screen Shot

It is important to teach young people not only how to manage relationships in real life but also in the digital world, and speak into some of the complexities that this world can uncover. Some of the teaching here would be into cyberbullying online, what it means to pause before you post and living with integrity online, sexting and also running a session on porn and its effects.

Getting it Right

When speaking into this theme, it is also important to teach into the breadth of relationships in our lives and the importance of doing these well. The following four topics might be sessions in a broader series or you may want to build a miniseries around each of these areas individually. However, when speaking to young people about relationships, it is vital that we teach into the areas of family, church community, friendships and also digital relationships online.

3 Giving and Serving

This theme unpacks what it looks like to give and serve others so that our lives become outwardly focused instead of just inwardly focused. Jesus is the ultimate example of serving. We want to think about how our giving and serving can point others to Jesus and how we can love others as we love ourselves.

Curriculum for Teaching

Give it Up

Young people can only give and serve when they realize how much they have to give. This theme is at the heart of this series. Here we would break down the areas where young people might be able to find resources to give. The sessions could cover the areas of giving time and money or of their gifts, but we have also used this teaching series to look at what they can give at Christmas and what it might look like to push against the tide of consumerism; however, that session is definitely best run in December!

The Church

Within this theme we can explore with young people what it looks like not only to be a part of but to serve the local church. Helpful sessions that we have run as a part of that series have covered 'Why the church?'—helping young people to see the importance of what it means to be a part of a church, the persecuted church, serving and where young people might be able to use their gifts in their local setting, and unity in the body.

Serve

In this series we look at what it means to love and serve others who might have less than we do. We would look at material poverty, relational poverty, spiritual poverty and environmental poverty and what it looks like to serve and stand alongside those who need our support.

The Servant King

We look to Jesus as our model of service and in this series we would do a biblical study of the person of Jesus and how he served those around him. Topics such as born to serve (Phil 2.1–13), embracing difference (John 4.4–30), upside-down service (John 13.1–17) and commitment (John 12. 20–26) are a few examples of what you might want to include.

4 Sharing the Gospel

We want to encourage the young people to own their faith and then share it with the friends and family around them. This theme explores the things that might hold us back from sharing faith and how we can be bold witnesses for Jesus.

Curriculum for Teaching

Go Viral

This series uses digital metaphors to explore what discipleship means and what it means to make disciples of others. The first session, 'React,' looks at our reaction to Jesus and how anything of any significance has to create some form of reaction, whether positive or negative. 'Subscribe' then looks at what it means to be a disciple and follow Jesus, 'Buffering' considers how we respond when things are tough or feel that they are on pause, and 'Share' covers our responsibility to make disciples of others.

Synchronize

Here we look at what it means to synchronize the three central stories that we encounter and bring them together into one story as we share our faith with our friends. We look at our own stories, what God has done and how we explain this to others; 'Your story,' therefore listening to and understanding the stories of our friends who do not know Jesus; 'God's story' and what Jesus has done for us; and then 'Our story,' what all of this coming together might look like. Youth for Christ have a YouTube series that accompanies this teaching that encourages young people to share their faith.

Evangelism

It can be that our teaching around evangelism is quite direct. A simple series that we have taught considers 'Who' God might want us to share our faith with and his heart for those that do not know him; 'What,' looking at what evangelism actually means and equally what it does not mean; 'How' should we do evangelism, talk about and demonstrate our faith and then look at inviting our friends to church; and 'So,' what does this mean for the way that we live, the urgency of the situation and the context in which young people live in the day to day.

Share

This series looks at what it means to prepare the ground for young people sharing their faith with their friends. We would cover the importance of praying for our friends, creating environments in our youth group that our friends who do not know Jesus want to be a part of, having confidence in sharing our faith and difficult questions, and how to keep going if our friends just are not interested.

5 Living Wisely

Making wise decisions is important and we want to encourage the young people to make life choices that will benefit them and honour God. This theme unpacks what the Bible has to say about wisdom and living for Jesus in all we do.

Curriculum for Teaching

Crash Barriers

We do not plan to make mistakes, we just do not plan not to. What does it mean to hit a crash barrier, rather than drift into oncoming traffic in the mistakes of our lives? We can use wisdom to put healthy boundaries in place. These boundaries must always be practical and measurable as well as accountable. Here we would unpack this concept, look at what our own individual disaster zones might be and how accountability can help us.

Life Hacks

Life hacks are simple changes that make a big difference, and this series looks at some simple concepts that help us to live wisely as we navigate life. These might look like peace, our attitude, forgiveness, new rules or living in grace, and dealing with exams.

Digital Detox

These sessions would consider what it looks like to live with wisdom in a digital age. Within this series you might look at how to conduct relationships wisely, what it means to be addicted to something and its effects (this might be porn, gaming or social media itself), popularity and comparison, and creating space for peace.

IDK: Tough Questions

IDK stands for 'I don't know.' Here we would look at what it means to have wisdom in the face of many difficult questions being asked about our faith. Some of these questions are age-old, such as 'Why would a loving God allow suffering' but others might be more difficult because we are not sure what the Bible says, or whether the Bible is still relevant in a modern world.

The World and Our Place in it

This generation is a globally connected generation, and not just concerned with connection to other people, but concerned with connection to the Earth itself. In Genesis humanity received the mandate to partner with God in taking the world somewhere, and this is a message that many of Generation Z feel keenly. There are many examples where young people themselves have leveraged their connectivity to be agents of change when it comes to looking after the planet, and it is vital for them to recognize that this is something that is on the heart of God.

6 Connecting with God

Our aim is to encourage the young people to develop a strong, personal relationship with Jesus. This theme focuses on how we can build spending time with God into our daily lives and the different ways that we can connect with God.

Curriculum for Teaching

Doing Bits

One way to approach connecting with God is by very practically giving the young people the tools to feed themselves. Here we might do a study of a different book of the Bible each week and look at doing this study in a different way that might connect with different learning styles. Some of the books that we have chosen to do that with are Ephesians, Philippians, Galatians and Colossians.

Deeper

Many young people struggle with Bible engagement so teaching into this specifically can be really helpful. You might take a session to teach the young people about how it came together, spend a session on reading the Bible and the difference that can make, very practically teach the young people how to have a devotional time, and then also talk to them about how to listen to, hear and discern the voice of God when they spend time with him.

Stripped Back

Teaching young people about wider spiritual disciplines is also important. We have run sessions on simplicity and simple living, on enabling 'airplane mode' and managing our time to spend time with God, and pursuing peace. You might also want to look at prayer and fasting or the discipline of worship and the difference it makes.

Blessed

This would also be an opportunity to teach into the spiritual gifts and how to use them. It might be that you want to structure sessions around each gift; you might want to vary the theory and the practice in these sessions, but doing this in line with your church's wider theology and teaching can be really helpful.

7 Character of God

Who we believe God is really matters. It affects how you pray or if you pray, how you interpret the world around you, how you treat others, and ultimately the bigger narrative for your life. In this teaching stream we look at the nature of who God is and also get the opportunity to ask some tough questions about how we interpret the world around us as a result of that.

Curriculum for Teaching

Why is God...

This is a really fun series to put together. If you go onto YouTube and type into the search bar, 'Why is God,' then a drop down will appear of the most searched phrases beginning with that question. Taking the top four or five of those statements and teaching into them can be a helpful and relevant way of answering some big questions.

It's Complicated

This series is a great opportunity to look at the persons of the Trinity. If you have unchurched young people in your group you will need to take them with you on this, but spending a session on the theology of the Trinity and then a session on God the Father, God the Son and God the Holy Spirit can be a really interesting time!

What's in a Name?

It can be helpful specifically to explore the nature of who God says he is. Take individual sessions to examine biblical examples of where we see God as provider, protector, judge, shepherd, shield or refuge, or any other of the names God attributes to himself, and help the young people to apply these elements of God's character to the circumstances that they might be facing in their immediate lives.

8 Identity

Young people grow up in a world with hundreds of voices telling them who they are and how they should live. It is very easy for the truth of God to be drowned out and for the foundation of who they are to be built on something other than the truth of God. Once we know who God is, we need to understand fully who God says we are so that our lives can be built upon our identity in Jesus.

Curriculum for Teaching

Defined

Young people often use the wrong markers to determine how they see themselves as an individual. Here, we can unpack some of the common areas where young people misplace their identity and measure it by the wrong thing. Some of the topics that you might want to look at could be popularity, our purpose—or what young people believe that to be, their sexuality and relationship status or their past. It is a great opportunity to speak truth into each of those areas.

New Rules

This series would specifically spend some time helping the young people to understand the spiritual freedom that is available to them when they choose to follow Jesus. Here you might spend a session looking at what that freedom means the other side of the cross, how some of the things of the past might or can hold us back and affect how we see ourselves, and then teach into how we deal with situations when they challenge our identity, and how we can pray into that.

Who Do You Say I am?

It's important to help young people not only understand but deeply know and feel what God speaks over them and who he says that they are. Over a number of sessions you can take passages of Scripture that describe these young people as loved, forgiven, chosen and filled with potential and help them to see what this means, not only for their own lives but for the lives of their friends who do not yet know Jesus.

The Journey of Everything

One way that a young person can understand who they are is by helping them to play their part in the wider narrative of humanity and their role in contributing to a story that spans eternity. You might want to begin by giving the young people an overview of the biblical narrative right through from Genesis to Revelation, spend some time in the next session thinking through creation and humanity's original purpose, then reflect upon the role of Jesus and our salvation in this bigger story, and conclude with helping the young people to understand our mission now.

Playing the Long Game

This list of curriculum ideas is by no means exhaustive, but merely here to act as a prompt, as you apply this to your own setting and consider Bible passages or topics that your young people will engage with. Most of these sessions are written and available on the Youth for Christ church resources site, but each time these key topics are taught they are taught in a different way with a different emphasis.

For example, Living Wisely might look at the Book of Daniel and how to live radically differently, with wisdom, in a culture that is very different from the one God intended. Or it might also look at the Book of Proverbs and study the principles of wisdom and how to apply the Bible to culture today. Equally, when you cover Relationships, this might be in the area of family, sex and relationships or friendships. How you do this and what you choose to cover has plenty of options behind it, but the important thing is that we are regularly, and intentionally, teaching into the topics that matter for the development of young people's faith.

7 Conclusion

As young people engage with a curriculum model over a prolonged period of time, the principles within become the fabric of their faith. My husband is the next generations pastor in our church and recently went and spent some time with one of the young people that has been in our church's ministry for the last seven years, the last four of which we were working from a curriculum. The young person, now a young adult, was doing well, but what struck my husband was that in conversation he was hearing back the principles that we had spent the four previous years teaching. Because of who I and my husband are our curriculum had a heavy posture towards evangelism and sharing your faith. One of the things we also spoke into regularly was the importance of time with God being something that remains in your diary when exam seasons hit. Andy sat and listened as, at the end of the first year of university, this guy had started taking some of the guys in his university halls to church and was making a commitment as exam season started, that the one thing he would not do was step back from not only attending church, but serving on the rotas that he was committed to. When things get busy, spending time with God becomes more crucial, not less. What a hero; teaching had become a part of his fabric.

As we look to disciple a generation, we should have in mind where we want them to be five or ten years after leaving our youth ministries and intentionally journey them towards that place as they navigate what the outworking of their faith looks like in an ever-changing world.

Notes

1 S Bullivant, *The 'No Religion' Population'of Britain,* https://www.stmarys.ac.uk/research/centres/benedict-xvi/docs/2017-may-no-religion-report.pdf (accessed 12 November 2019).

2 L Singlehurst, *Sowing, Reaping, Keeping* (London: IVP, 2006).

3 J Harris, *The Nurture Assumption* (New York: Free Press, 1998).

4 For example: R Neighbour, *A How-to Guide for Mentoring another Christian* (Houston, TX: Touch Publications, 2001).

5 N Pearcey, *Finding Truth: 5 Principles for Unmasking Atheism, Secularism, and Other God Substitutes* (Colorado Springs, CO: David C Cook Publishing Company, 2019).

6 D Kinnaman, *You Lost Me: Why Young Christians Are Leaving Church...and Rethinking Faith* (Grand Rapids, MI: Baker Books, 2016).

7 K Powell, B Griffin and C Crawford, *Sticky Faith Youth Worker Edition* (Grand Rapids, MI: Zondervan, 2011).

8 See https://resources.yfc.co.uk/